THE SPACES IN BETWEEN

For my little bean – J.K.

For Mum – M.T.

BIG PICTURE PRESS

This edition published in the UK in 2024 by Big Picture Press.
First published in the UK in 2023 by Big Picture Press,
an imprint of Bonnier Books UK,
4th Floor, Victoria House,
Bloomsbury Square, London, WC1B 4DA
Owned by Bonnier Books
Sveavägen 56, Stockholm, Sweden
www.bonnierbooks.co.uk

Text copyright © 2023 by Jaspreet Kaur
Illustration copyright © 2023 by Manjit Thapp
Design copyright © 2023 by Big Picture Press

1 3 5 7 9 10 8 6 4 2

All rights reserved

ISBN 978-1-78741-935-3 (Hardback)
ISBN 978-1-80078-705-6 (Paperback)

This book was typeset in Catalina Clemente.
The illustrations were created digitally.

Edited by Joanna McInerney
Designed by Olivia Cook
Production by Neil Randles

Printed in China

THE SPACES IN BETWEEN

Jaspreet Kaur Manjit Thapp

BPP

The city can make you feel ANXIOUS.
The city can make you feel SHY.
But there are lots of things that might help,
you just have to use your eyes!

Big dogs bark and people CHATTER.
The thundering trains go CLITTER CLATTER.

Your heart is **THUMPING**, mouth goes *dry*.
It seems there's nowhere you can hide!

But in the BIG and BUSTLING city, you'll find the spaces in between . . .

If you look hard enough, you might just find . . .

... the secret places no one else has seen.

... special spaces to quieten your mind.

Even on your high street, there are spaces you can spot. It could be your local library, or your favourite shop.

There are **happy** little moments,
happening all around.
Colours to spot, things to see
and **peace** to be found.

If you listen closely, you might hear a familiar tune. It's the jingly jangly ice-cream van, serving smiles all afternoon!

Walking with your cone,
you might spot another space.
A **beautiful** little pond,
behind a set of big green gates.

You could sit and eat your cone
on the benches in the park.
Skip through bright and crunchy leaves
that decorate the path.

High, high up, you can see all of the sights. So much nature hidden in the surrounding heights.

Yes, in the BIG and BUSTLING city, you'll find the spaces in between . . .

... the secret places no one else has seen.

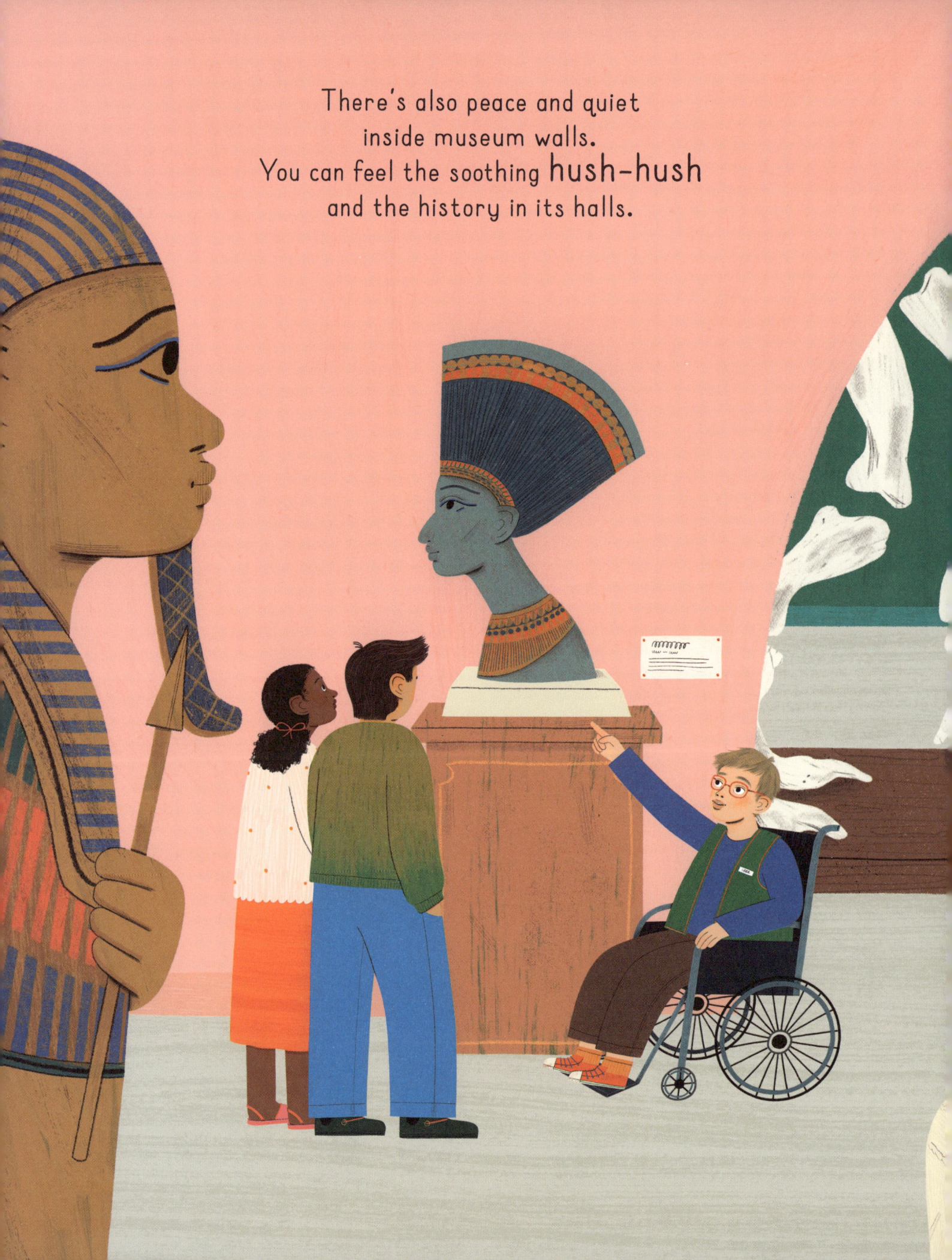

It's like a secret world when you first walk through the doors. Amongst the spooky mummies, maps and the fearsome dinosaurs.

If the Tube is feeling just a bit too busy and **loud**, You can always find a way to escape from the crowd.

Stand beside the platform and watch the trains come and go. Wave at the conductor, and they might just wave *hello!*

It's time to head home,
the weather has turned nippy.
Notice the twinkling lights in the
big and bustling city.

Slurping a hot chocolate while
people are passing by,
Friendly faces here and there
greet you with a smile.

As you fall asleep, let yourself dream, of all those calming little spaces in between...

...the secret places no one else has seen.

MINDFULNESS IN THE CITY

It's normal to sometimes feel overwhelmed in a busy, noisy, crowded space. The next time you are feeling worried, you might want to try some of these activities that could relieve symptoms of stress and anxiety.

Breathing Exercises
To prepare yourself for a busy day, take a few moments in the morning to take a deep breath in through your nose and slowly release out through your mouth. Repeat.

Send Friendly Wishes
Think about your day ahead and who you might meet. You might want to send a nice wish to one of your friends or family, such as 'may they be happy today', or 'may they be well today'.

Stretch
When we are stressed, our muscles can get tense. Pretend you are a dog who has just woken from a nap. Lie face down, then press your palms against the floor as you lift your upper body. Tilt your head up a little to stretch your back.

Notice Nature
Nature is all around us, even in urban spaces. See if you can spot some flowers poking up through the pavement, or a bird nesting high above the city. What else can you find?

Mindful Smelling
Some smells can make our brains release happy chemicals. While walking around the city, see if you can smell any of the following: coffee, freshly baked bread, a pine tree, cut grass.

Paint a Picture
Drawing and colouring helps us to relax. Think about your day and draw something nice you may have seen.

Listen to Music
If the city is feeling a little noisy, you might want to take some headphones with you and listen to some calming music. Or, perhaps you might want to block out sounds and not listen to anything at all.

Eat Something Delicious
Sometimes when we are anxious we don't feel hungry. But eating something tasty will make us feel better. Pick up a healthy snack, and eat it slowly.

Write in a Diary
Writing can help us to process what we are thinking and feeling. You might want to record something in a diary, or maybe write a story where you can use your imagination.

Have a Chat
It really helps to talk to loved ones about how we are feeling. Spend some time with a parent, teacher or friend and talk about your day.

Sleep and Rest
When we are tired, we can become stressed. Our brains need time to relax. Find a bedtime routine that works for you, whether that's reading a story or taking a warm bath.

ABOUT THE AUTHOR

Jaspreet Kaur, also known by her online name 'Behind the Netra', is an award-winning teacher, spoken-word poet and author from London. Jaspreet is also a judge for the annual Queen's Commonwealth Essay Competition and the prestigious Roundhouse Poetry Slam. When she's not writing, Jaspreet likes spending her time reading, cooking, travelling and spending time with family. She has two fluffy cats, five chickens and loves to go for long walks in nature with her husband and her dog, Heera.

ABOUT THE ILLUSTRATOR

Manjit Thapp is an illustrator from the UK whose work combines digital and traditional media. Her favourite things to draw are female characters, and her illustrations are inspired by colours, patterns, nature and everyday feelings. In her spare time, she loves reading and doodling ideas for future drawings.